Salvation History
Story Time

Move and Play with Scripture

Katie Warner
Illustrated by Amy Rodriguez

OSV kids
Huntington, Indiana

Nihil Obstat
Msgr. Michael Heintz, Ph.D.
Censor Librorum

Imprimatur
✠ Kevin C. Rhoades
Bishop of Fort Wayne-South Bend
May 30, 2023

The *Nihil Obstat* and *Imprimatur* are official declarations that a book is free from doctrinal or moral error. It is not implied that those who have granted the *Nihil Obstat* and *Imprimatur* agree with the contents, opinions, or statements expressed.

28 27 26 25 24 23 1 2 3 4 5 6 7 8 9

Our Sunday Visitor Publishing Division, Our Sunday Visitor, Inc., 200 Noll Plaza, Huntington, IN 46750; www.osv.com; 1-800-348-2440

ISBN: 978-1-63966-036-0 (Inventory No. T2788)
1. JUVENILE NONFICTION—Religion—Bible Stories—General.
2. JUVENILE NONFICTION—Religious—Christian—Inspirational.
3. RELIGION—Christianity—Catholic.

eISBN: 978-1-63966-037-7
LCCN: 2023942639

Cover and interior design: Lindsey Riesen
Cover and interior art: Amy Rodriguez

PRINTED IN TURKEY

For my Peter, may God's Word always be a lamp to your feet and a light to your path. – KW

Dedicated to my beloved mom, Maria Guadalupe. Thank you for sharing your deep faith and love with me and our family. – AR

Contents

A Note from the Author

(to the Adult Readers)

Joy!

This is what I want my children to experience in their walk with Jesus in the little years.

This fun and interactive book aims to bring Scripture to life for young children, by telling pieces of the story of salvation history in a dynamic way and inviting the children to be a part of the adventure: making animal noises and marching, praying and singing, dancing and imagining along the way.

This journey through Scripture should bring laughter, smiles, and *joy* to your Bible time, hopefully planting seeds for an engaging relationship with Scripture that lasts a lifetime.

Each story is taken from a different season in salvation history, taking you and your young ones on a journey from creation through the life of Christ and into the age of the Church.

This book contains just a sampling of stories! But diving into these selected scenes allows children to see that there are adventure stories throughout the whole Bible, all of which come together to tell the grand saga of God's uncontainable love for the world.

The Bible is far from boring. This storybook is meant to help remind us of that — to help us step into the shoes of the cast of characters in Sacred Scripture, experience their trials and triumphs, and see our own lives reflected in these stories, growing in knowledge, trust, love, and *joy* as we go. Prompts to converse, interact, and play with the children are sprinkled throughout these stories. This type of tangible, kinesthetic learning will help children better encounter and remember these Bible stories.

You will also find suggested Bible passages that accompany each read-aloud. Taking advantage of these readings will help your child hear and treasure God's *living and active* Word — straight from the source. Even if you don't read those "deep dive" verses every time, try reading them at some point with your children, so they can benefit from hearing the actual words of Scripture!

Let us not forget, God has "hidden these things from the wise and understanding and revealed them to infants" (Mt 11:25)! Our children hunger for God's Word as much as we do, and their understanding often surpasses what we could imagine.

May you have fun and meaningful interactions with your little ones as you study the Bible together ... all for the greater glory of God!

— Katie Warner

Deep Dive: Genesis 1:1–31

Adults: Have your child grab some animal friends for this story. Stuffed animals, animal toys, hand-drawn pictures of animals or magazine cutouts ... whatever animal friends they can find!

1

In the Beginning

Let's dive into the Bible together and journey *way* back to the creation of the world. In the beginning, God created the heavens and the earth. He made the light, the land and the seas, the sun, the moon, the stars, the fish and the birds, and the land animals.

Isn't God so creative?

God saw all that He had made and it was *good*. But God created something extra special on the sixth day. Something *very good*.

Do you know what He created?

People! He saved the best for last!

God made us in his image and likeness and He gave people a special role in his creation. He even gave people dominion, or control, over the animals. He allowed Adam to name the animals, showing his authority over them. **What is your favorite animal that God made? Can you make that animal's sound or pretend to be that animal? Show me!**

Naming is an action of great power in Scripture! Names are still important to us today. What is your name? Do you know what it means? **Now, pretend to be Adam living way back in the time of creation. March your animals in front of you, and as they pass by, give each of them a name!**

That was quite an adventure exploring the early world God created. Do you know what God did on the seventh day? He rested. **Can you and your animals lie down and snore?**

While you are resting, I want to tell you a little about what happened next. Unfortunately, this perfect life in the garden didn't last forever. Adam and his wife, Eve, disobeyed God. We call this moment the Fall. The ugliness of sin entered the beauty of God's creation and history was changed forever.

But God did not abandon His creatures to the consequences of sin. He had a marvelous plan to show His people — to show us — exactly how much He loves us.

Thank you, God, for the gift of Your Holy Word today.

Deep Dive: Genesis 37

Adults: Have your children put on a special outfit for this story! Let them pick out something really fun, colorful, or crazy, or even a costume! Get creative!

2

The Patriarchal Age

Let's journey *way* back to the time of the Patriarchs, the "fathers" of the Israelites, the people to whom God chose to reveal himself in a special way. This is the time when Abraham, Isaac, and Jacob lived.

Jacob, one of the patriarchs, had twelve sons. Jacob loved his son, Joseph, in a unique way and made him a long, decorative robe. This was a pretty special outfit — just like the special outfit you picked to wear — and it made Joseph's brothers jealous. **Can you show me your outfit? Walk or dance**

around in the fancy clothes you chose.

Well, it wasn't just the special robe that made Joseph's brothers angry. Joseph also had dreams — dreams that meant his family would bow down to him someday. **Can you bow like the sheaves, sun, moon, and stars bowed down in Joseph's dreams?** The sheaves, sun, moon, and stars represented Joseph's brothers bowing before him.

This was just too much for his jealous brothers, so they plotted to get rid of Joseph. They came up with a plan and they shared it with each other.

Adults: Play "telephone" with however many children are present. Whisper the "plan" into the child's ear and then instruct him/her to whisper into a sibling's ear and so on, or back to the adult reader if no other children are present. Here's the plan: **"Let's sell Joseph into slavery!"**

What a wicked plan! Jealousy is a sin, and one sin can lead you into even greater sin ... and that's what happened to Joseph's brothers. They were so jealous that they sold him into slavery and Joseph ended up in Egypt, far away from his home and family.

The good news is that God can always bring good out of evil. He can bring happy endings to our bad plans. Joseph became a great leader in Egypt. He later forgave his brothers and even helped them when they were in need! **Can you give hugs to those you are reading with, like Joseph hugged and reunited with his brothers?**

Jacob's family, including Joseph and his brothers, settled in Egypt, where they lived for the next several hundred years ... but we will find out soon that the Israelites aren't going to want to *stay* in Egypt.

Thank you, God, for the gift of Your Holy Word today.

Deep Dive: Exodus 3:1–4:23

3

The Exodus from Egypt

Let's journey back to the time of the Exodus.

After Joseph and his brothers settled in Egypt, the Israelites (Jacob's descendants) eventually became slaves to the Egyptians. The Pharaoh, concerned about the growing number of Israelites, made an evil decision to get rid of all the Israelite baby boys by having them thrown into the river.

The Bible tells the story of one baby boy who was saved from being killed. His mother put him in a little basket and set him floating on the river, watched over by his sister, Miriam. **Can**

you guess the baby boy's name? Moses!

Moses grew up as a prince in Pharaoh's household. He later ran away from Egypt and became a shepherd. **Can you make the sound of a sheep?**

One day, while Moses was watching those bleating sheep, he saw a bush that was on fire, but it wasn't burning up. **What kind of a face would you make if you saw a bush with giant flames coming from it? Show me.**

Well, the story gets even more surprising because then *God* started talking to Moses from the bush! God told Moses He wanted him to help set the Israelites free from slavery in Egypt and bring them to a land where they would worship God alone. Moses thought this was a pretty big job and wasn't sure he'd be a very good leader, but God was with Moses, and gave Moses all of the tools he needed to carry out God's plan.

Unfortunately, Pharoah had a hard heart and did *not* want to cooperate with God's plan, so God sent plagues on Egypt to show His power and get Pharaoh's attention. Some of the plagues included frogs, flies, and darkness. **Can you hop like a frog? Can you buzz around like a pesky fly? Can you cover your eyes and listen to the next part of the story in darkness?**

Well, the last plague, in which all the firstborn Egyptian children died, convinced Pharoah to let God's people go. And though Pharoah changed his mind again, the Israelites did *see the light* of freedom from Egypt **(uncover your eyes now!)**, and they celebrated with singing and dancing. **Let's have our own dance party now to remember the Israelites rejoicing in their freedom from Egypt.**

Thank you, God, for the gift of Your Holy Word today.

Deep Dive: Numbers 14

Adults: Before reading, hide objects for your children to hunt for at the end of the story. Bonus points if you are able to hide milk, honey, grapes, or figs to recall the Israelites' real experience!

4

Roaming in the Wilderness

Let's journey back to the time when the Israelites wandered in the desert after leaving Egypt.

The Israelites, though free from the Egyptians, still had a *lot* to learn about trusting in the God who freed them as they journeyed toward the promised land. God continued to care for the Israelites during this time, giving them food, water, His presence in the Tabernacle, and the Ten Commandments (God's laws for teaching His people how to love Him and love others). **Can you count to 10 for the Ten Commandments? Now, can you**

pretend to eat and drink like the Israelites eating and drinking the manna, quail, and water sent from God?

The Lord always provides for His people!

God kept reassuring the Israelites of His presence and His desire to bless them. He even gave Moses and Aaron a special blessing to say over the people. **Can you fold your hands in prayer and bow your head? I'm going to pray the same special blessing over you!**

"The Lord bless you and keep you:

"The Lord make his face to shine upon you, and be gracious to you:

"The Lord lift up his countenance upon you, and give you peace" (Nm 6:24–26).

When the Israelites reached the Promised Land, Moses sent twelve scouts to explore the land that "flow[ed] with milk and honey" (Nm 14:8). They came back forty days later with grapes and figs ... but they also came back afraid of the people living in the land. **Let's go on our own scouting adventure! Can you "survey the land" and find _______?**

Though two brave scouts, Caleb and Joshua, encouraged the others to continue trusting God, many Israelites complained and doubted God's care for them. So that the Israelites would learn to trust Him, God allowed them to wander in the desert for forty years before entering the Promised Land.

Thank you, God, for the gift of Your Holy Word today.

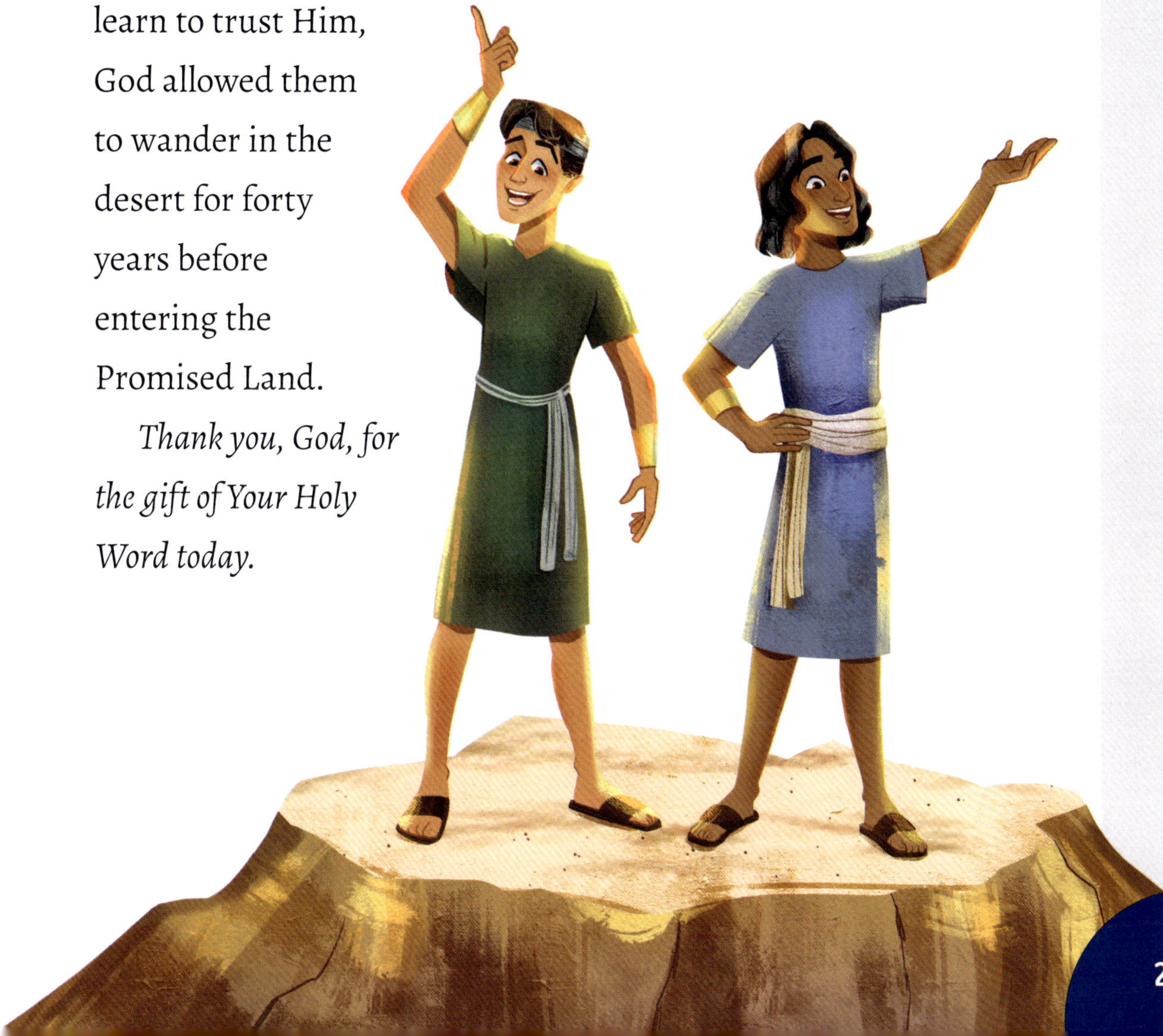

5

Conquering the Promised Land

Let's go back to the time when the Israelites *finally* entered the Promised Land.

Last time, we met Joshua, one of the brave Israelites who trusted in God even when everyone else struggled to. Well, Joshua continued trusting God and God promised Joshua that He would be with him wherever he went. God's words to Joshua are encouraging for us, too. **Can you repeat the words of Joshua 1:9 after me?**

Be strong and of good courage;
be not frightened,
neither be dismayed;
for the LORD your God is with you
wherever you go.

Adults: Consider memorizing this verse as a family this month!

It was time for the Israelites to enter the Promised Land. Joshua sent spies to check out the city of Jericho, and the spies came back letting him know that the people of Jericho were scared of the Israelites.

So the Israelites crossed the Jordan River, which miraculously dried up for their safe crossing, and headed toward the tall, strong wall surrounding Jericho. It was time to take the city with God's instructions and help.

The priests led the way with the Ark of the Covenant, and the Israelites began marching around the city. *Adults: Pick a couch or table that you can march around for the next part of the story.* **Let's march around the table/couch now as I continue reading! Can you march while shouting with your best "inside voice"?**

The Israelites marched every day for six days. Then, on the seventh day, they marched around the city seven times, while the priest blew trumpets and the Israelites shouted.

Do you know what happened next? The walls of the city

came crumbling down! The Israelites went in and rested after their long journey. God had kept His promise, as He always does.

Thank you, God, for the gift of Your Holy Word today.

Deep Dive: 1 Kings 8:6–20

6

The Kingdom of Israel

Let's journey back to the time when the Israelites were ruled by kings.

Last time, we entered the Promised Land with Joshua and the Israelites after a *long* journey to get there. When Joshua died, they no longer had a leader. Do you think things went smoothly for them without a good leader?

No. The people should have looked to God as their leader, but instead they tried to lead themselves without His help. **Let's stand up. Close your eyes. Now, take a step. Good. What if I told**

you to keep walking with your eyes closed, all around the house? What do you think would happen?

Open your eyes and let's sit down.

The Israelites tried living without good leadership, and it made a big mess of things, like trying to navigate your way in the dark. Twelve judges took turns leading Israel. Things didn't get much better, because the Israelites were stuck in a cycle of sinning and forgetting to follow *God* as their leader.

Now the Israelites wanted a king to rule them, but who really wanted to be their king?

Yes, God! He wanted to be their one, true king — a king that was way better than all the other nation's kings. But God allowed them to have a kingdom.

The first king of Israel was Saul, who was a pretty flawed man. But David, the second king, was a man after God's heart. He wanted to build God a beautiful house, but God wanted to build a different kind of "house" for *David*. He made a promise — a covenant — with David, that He would establish for him a royal family that would last forever. We call it the "house of David," and Jesus would come from this holy kingdom many generations later.

That special house David wanted to build for God was indeed built! David's son Solomon built God a beautiful temple in Jerusalem. The glory of the Lord filled the Temple and all of Israel loved to worship there. **If you could make a house for God, what would it look like?**

Let's think about Solomon building a beautiful house for God while we build our own structure now with blocks, Legos, or other building supplies!

Thank you, God, for the gift of Your Holy Word today.

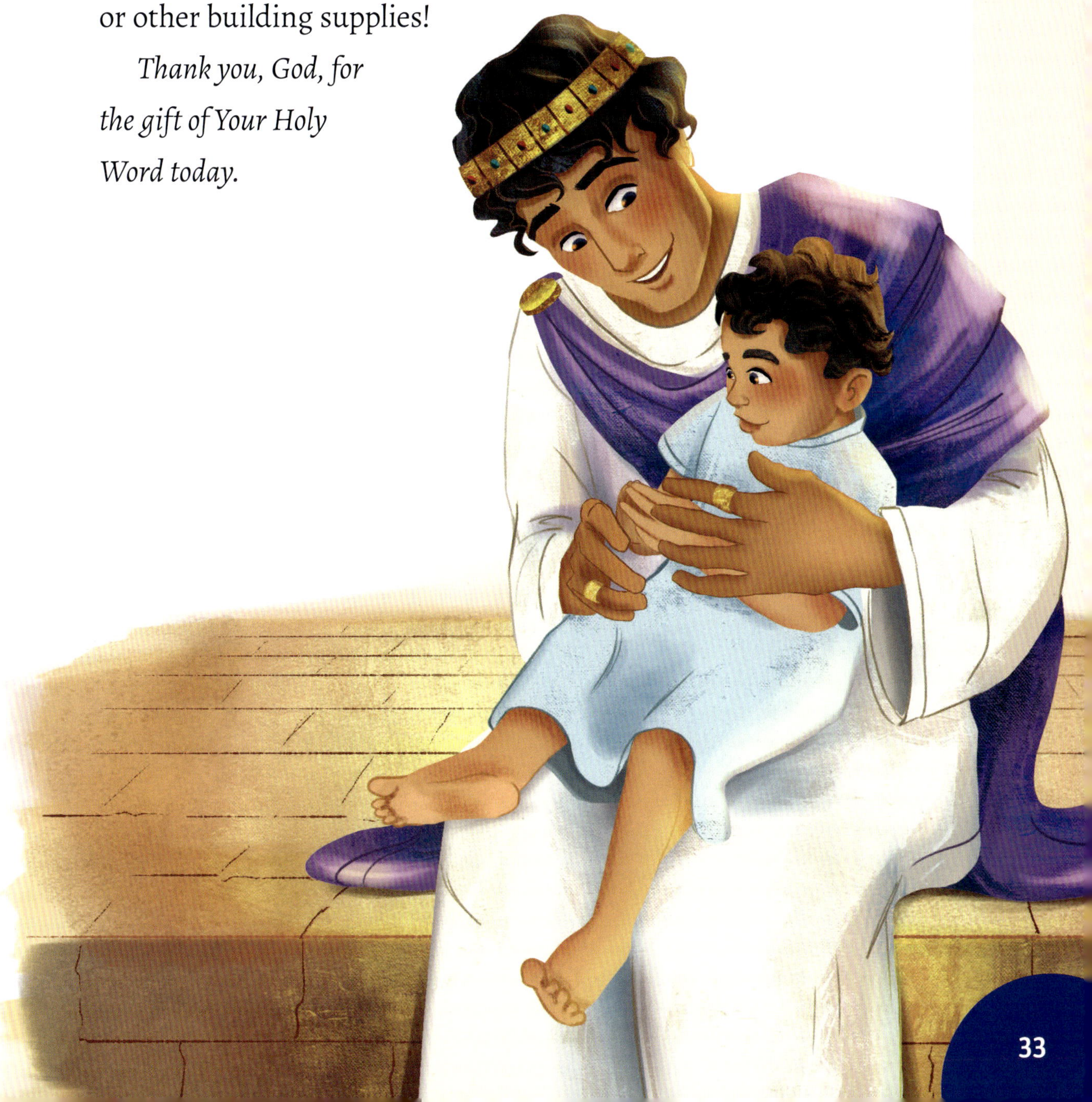

Deep Dive: 2 Kings 2:1–22

Adults, give a blank piece of paper to each child as the story begins. Each child will also need to wear a cape. If you don't have a costume cape, use a towel, play scarf, or some item that can be wrapped and tied like a cape.

7

The Kingdom Breaks Apart

Let's journey back to another hard time in Israel's history—the time when the kingdom divided.

We already learned that Israel had become a kingdom. Well, the Israelites were not faithful to God, and after King Solomon died, the kingdom split in two. **Can you rip your paper in half?**

Are you sad when things you love break? This broken kingdom was a sad thing for God's people, and a lot of bad kings reigned in both the North and the South.

But God never stops trying to make things good for His children. He sent prophets to give messages of repentance and hope to His chosen people.

One of those prophets was Elijah. Elijah worked hard to deliver God's messages and en-

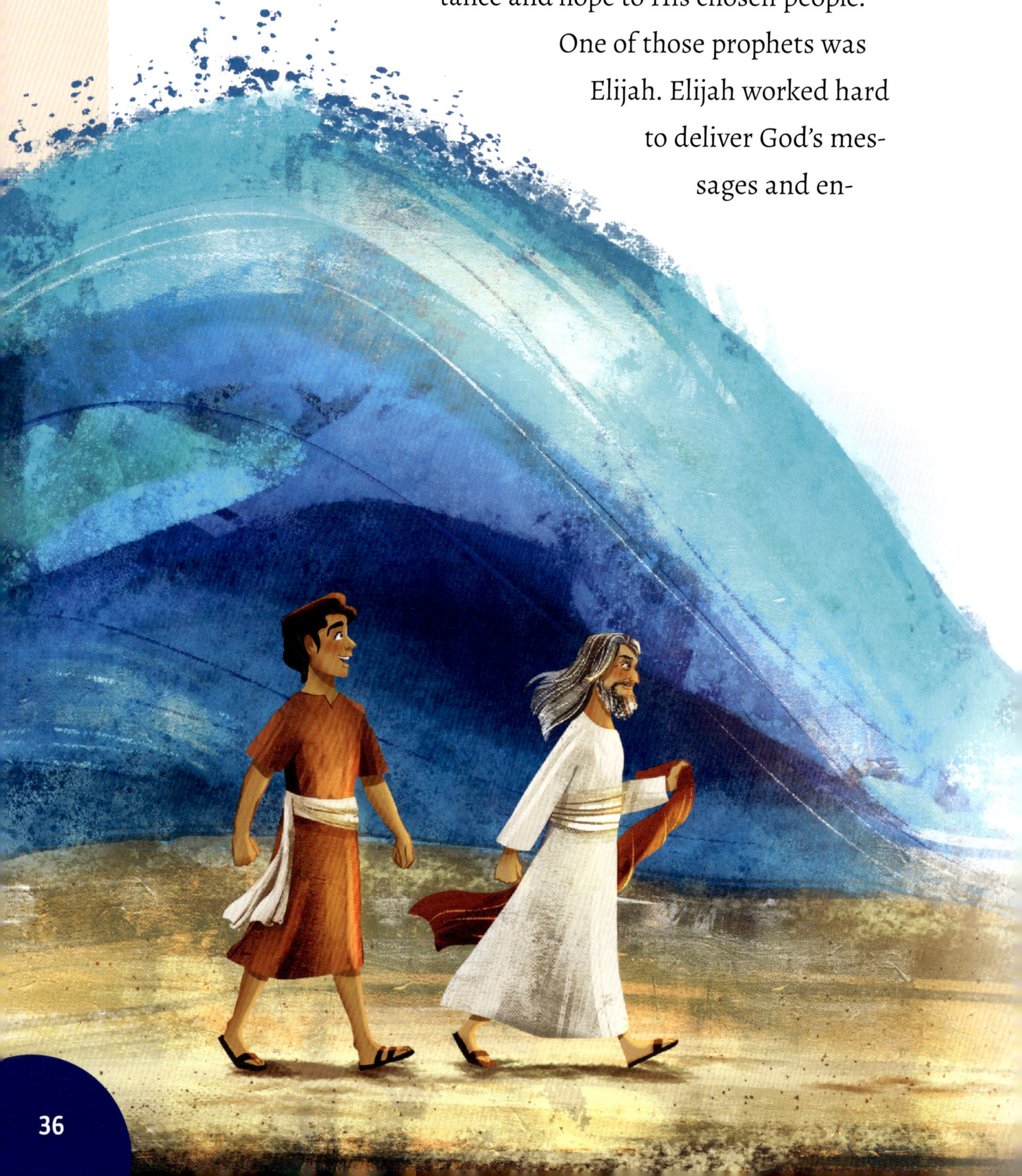

courage the people and the kings to change their evil ways. His life involved a lot of traveling and hiding, but it also involved a lot of miracles.

He multiplied food, raised a boy from the dead, and helped defeat the evil prophets and their false gods. After such a defeat, the people knelt down and worshiped the one true God. **Can you kneel down and cheer "The LORD, he is God" as the Israelites did (in 1 Kings 18:39)?**

Elijah grew older and God chose a man named Elisha to carry on his mission.

Elijah and Elisha walked by the Jordan River one day. Elijah took off his cape, rolled it up, and he hit the river with it. **Take off your cape now! Roll your cape up! Hit the ground with your cape!** The water divided and Elijah and Elisha crossed on the dry land that appeared. Suddenly, a chariot of fire came from the sky and picked up Elijah, taking him off into heaven!

What do you think Elisha's face looked like watching that happen?

Elisha picked up the cape **(grab your cape and put it on as Elisha did!)** and continued Elijah's work, doing miracles and telling people and kings to repent and to follow God.

Thank you, God, for the gift of Your Holy Word today.

8

The Israelites Leave Home

Let's journey back to the period of exile.

Last time, we learned that after the kingdom of Israel was divided, many bad kings ruled and the people struggled to obey God. Sadly, God's people did not listen to the prophets God sent to help them, and both kingdoms were taken over by foreign powers.

Many people were forced to leave their homes and were sent off to distant places. How would you feel if you were kicked out of your home? **Can you march away with your head low, like the Jews did?**

It was so sad, but it gets worse! The king of Babylon, one of the powerful foreign rulers, had his men go to that beautiful Temple that Solomon had built in Jerusalem and they destroyed it. They broke, stole, and burned the things in the Temple. Can you imagine someone destroying your whole room? Tearing apart, smashing, and taking things that matter to you? This happened to God's house!

Thankfully, God still brought comfort to His people after this tragedy. He sent more prophets to remind them of His care.

One of those prophets was Daniel, a faithful and wise young man who ended up working in the palace of the king of Babylon. When Daniel, with God's help, was able to interpret the king's dream about a statue — **can you be as still as a statue?** — the king even made Daniel a ruler!

Well, some of the officers of the king did not like Daniel. They caught Daniel praying to God. This was against a bad, new law in Babylon that required people to worship the king alone. Daniel's punishment was to be thrown into a den of lions! **Can you make the sound of an angry, hungry lion?**

Daniel was surrounded by angry, hungry lions when an angel came to save him by shutting the lions' mouths! **Can you snap your jaw shut like the lions' mouths were shut tight**

by God's angel?

God saved Daniel *and* changed many hearts that day. Over time, God's people remembered how much they loved and needed God, and they hoped and prayed they could one day go home, back to Jerusalem.

Thank you, God, for the gift of Your Holy Word today.

Deep Dive: Nehemiah 8

Adults, have some instruments nearby before you begin the story. If you don't have child instruments, feel free to use kitchen supplies or whatever you have on hand to make a simple drum or noisemaker.

9

Returning Home to Jerusalem

Let's journey back to the time when the Jewish people returned from exile and went back to their homes in Jerusalem.

As hard as the exile was, God never left his people and He brought them comfort when they were struggling. God is always with you, too, in all the hard and happy moments of your own life. He remained with the descendants of Abraham we've been following throughout salvation history, who are now called the Jews after the tribe of Judah.

One day, the king told the Jewish exiles to *go home*. Can you imagine how excited the Jews must have been? **Show me how excited!**

They were probably dancing and singing and laughing with joy to return to Jerusalem and rebuild the Temple, God's house, that had been destroyed.

So that's just what they did. They rebuilt the walls around Jerusalem, which had been broken, to make the city safe again. **Can you stack blocks and make a big, tall wall?**

Once the wall was rebuilt, Ezra the priest read to all the people from the Book of the Law that God had given to Moses. This was such a joyous experience for the Jewish people and they celebrated by singing and playing instruments! **Can you grab your instrument and play a joyful song of thanksgiving, like the Jews did to praise God?**

God had kept His promise to restore and bless His people.

Does God always keep his promises?

YES!

Let me hear you again...does God always keep His promises?

YES!!!

What a faithful God.

Thank you, God, for the gift of Your Holy Word today.

Deep Dive: 2 Maccabees 7 (Be aware of sensitive content.)

Adults: Before beginning, have a map of Europe accessible in print or on your phone, computer, or tablet.

10

The Maccabean Revolt

Let's journey back to the time when yet another world power was persecuting the Jews. God's people were no strangers to persecution, right? But we will meet some heroes during this time who show us how we can always stay true to our faith, no matter what.

After the Jews returned home from their time in exile and began living and worshiping in Jerusalem again, Greece grew in influence around the world, spreading their culture and religion. **Can you help me find the country of Greece on the map?**

The Greeks believed in many gods. **Can you wiggle all your fingers in the air? How about some of your toes? The Greeks believed in even more gods than that!**

But how many did the Jews have? Show me the number. That's right. ONE.

Well, the Greeks wanted the Jews to worship their gods and do other things contrary to their faith, but the faithful Jews refused. Jews like the priest Mattathias and his son, Judas Maccabeus, defended God's laws and fought against the Greek persecution.

The Bible shares the story of a particularly heroic family who stood up for their Jewish faith.

There was a mother who raised her sons to be faithful to God. The Greek ruler of the area, Antiochus, ordered this mother and her seven boys to worship a statue and eat pork, a food Jews were not supposed to eat. They had to make a choice: obey God or obey man.

The first son chose. **Repeat after me: "I obey God!"**

The second son chose. **Repeat after me: "I obey God!"**

The third son chose. **Repeat after me: "I obey God!"**

The fourth son chose. **Repeat after me: "I obey God!"**

The fifth son chose. **Repeat after me: "I obey God!"**

The sixth son chose. **Repeat after me: "I obey God!"**

The seventh and last son chose. **Repeat after me: "I obey God!"**

Isn't that inspiring? Not a single son denied his faith, even when faced with death. Finally, even their brave, faithful, encouraging mother was killed. We call these heroic people who die for their faith martyrs. May we always obey God and stay true to our faith like they did, no matter what.

Thank you, God, for the gift of Your Holy Word today.

Deep Dive: Luke 2:1–40

11

The Coming of Jesus

Let's journey back to the time that all of history, all of God's people, and all of creation had been waiting for ... the coming of Jesus.

It's been a long journey to get here. God's people have experienced much oppression, but no bondage was greater than their enslavement to sin. Thankfully, since the time of Adam and Eve, when sin mangled God's original and beautiful story, God had a plan to set His people free and to show us how much He loves us.

God demonstrated over and over again, that He always

keeps his ________. **Can you finish the sentence?**

Yes, God always keeps His promises, and this answered promise — when God sent His Son to reunite us with himself — was the best one yet.

God chose a holy young woman named Mary to be the Mother of Jesus, and she responded with these beautiful words that we remember today as her "fiat" — her "yes" to God.

Repeat her fiat after me: "Behold, I am the handmaid of the Lord, let it be to me according to your word" (Lk 1:38).

Mary and Joseph, her husband, traveled to a town named Bethlehem where Mary gave birth to baby Jesus in humble surroundings. **Did God come into the world as a strong, middle-aged king? No!** He came as a baby!

Can you make the sound of a crying baby?

Can you show me how you eat? How you dance? How you sleep? How you hug? Jesus did ALL of those things as He grew up, just like you are doing now.

He was like YOU in all things, except sin. He wanted to show how much He loves you and how close He is to you, by becoming like you.

The story of Jesus coming into the world, dying, and rising again so that we could live with Him forever in heaven is the greatest story ever told. As God's people living in the world today, we must always keep His story alive by sharing it with others.

Thank you, God, for the gift of Your Holy Word today.

Deep Dive: Luke 2:41–52

12

Jesus, the Youth

Let's journey to the time of Jesus' childhood. We read about His birth and talked about how He grew up doing a lot of the things that you do, but there are only a few glimpses that Scripture gives us into Jesus' early years. Let's experience one of those childhood moments together: the last story about Jesus as a young boy.

Jesus, along with Mary and Joseph, had traveled to Jerusalem for the feast of Passover, just like they did every year. Do you remember the story about Moses and the Israelites being freed from slavery in Egypt? That's the occasion that Jesus and His family, along with many other Jews, were remembering and celebrating.

Remember, they didn't have cars back then, only animals and their own two feet, so their travels involved a *lot* of walking. **Can you walk in place while I read this next part?**

After celebrating the Passover, everyone began heading home to Nazareth, but on the way, Mary and Joseph realized that Jesus wasn't with the group!

Mary and Joseph rushed back to Jerusalem and began searching everywhere for Jesus. Can you imagine losing the Son of God? Thankfully, they found Him in the Temple, listening to the elders, asking them questions, and giving his own wise answers, much to the amazement of those around Him.

Mary and Joseph were so relieved. **Can you let out a big sigh of relief?** When they asked Jesus why He had done this, Jesus answered them, "Did you not know that I must be in my Father's house?" (Lk 2:49).

Like a good son, Jesus was obedient to His parents and to His Heavenly Father and went home to Nazareth, where He grew in age and wisdom. He helped His mother Mary, learned carpentry from Saint Joseph **(can you pretend to use a saw?)**, and prayed and studied God's law **(can you pretend to read a Bible in your hands?).**

Thank you, God, for the gift of Your Holy Word today. **To remember the story of the Finding of Jesus in the Temple, let's play a game of hide and seek. I'll count while you hide, and then find you like Mary and Joseph found Jesus that day!**

Deep Dive: Matthew 13:31–50

13

Jesus, the Teacher

Let's journey back to the time of Jesus' ministry. As we learned in our last story, Jesus grew up with Mary and Joseph and lived a quiet life in Nazareth. When He was about 30 years old, Jesus was baptized, tempted by the devil in the desert, and began His public ministry preaching the kingdom of God.

But He didn't want to do this ministry work alone. He chose twelve apostles to be his closest friends and accompany Him on this mission. **Let's list the apostles together. You can**

repeat their names after me: Peter, Andrew, James, John, Philip, Bartholomew, Matthew, Thomas, James, Thaddeus, Simon, and Judas. Do you recognize any of these names? Can you tell me anything you already know about any of these apostles? These twelve men learned so much from Jesus, were loved deeply by him, and were with him as he taught crowds of people wherever he traveled. Some of Jesus' teachings were surprising to the people of his day. In the Beatitudes, part of Jesus' Sermon on the Mount in Matthew 5, Jesus taught that those who are poor, meek,

mourning, and persecuted are *blessed*! **Can you pretend to put on a crown like the saints who inherit the kingdom of heaven?** Jesus even taught people to love their enemies and to pray for them! **Can you show me your prayer hands?**

Jesus was also known for telling his disciples parables, or stories, about what the kingdom of God is like. He told them the kingdom of heaven is like a tiny mustard seed that grows into a mighty tree. **Can you pretend to be a seed that springs up into a big, tall tree?** He told them that the kingdom of heaven is like leaven, or yeast,that makes dough rise. **Can you pretend to knead bread dough with your hands?** He told them that the kingdom of heaven is like treasure hidden in a field. **Can you show me the face you would make if you found hidden treasure?** He told them that the kingdom of heaven is like a net that was thrown into the sea and gathered fish of every kind. **Can you pretend to go fishing?**

Through all of these parables, Jesus prepared His disciples' hearts for the kingdom of God. Many people opened their hearts and fell in love with Jesus, while others worried about His growing popularity and were disturbed by his surprising lessons.

Thank you, God, for the gift of Your Holy Word today.

Deep Dive: Matthew 8:5–13

14

Jesus, the Miracle Worker and Healer

Let's journey back to the time of Jesus' ministry. Our last story showed us how Jesus was a remarkable teacher, but it wasn't just His teaching that made the word about Jesus spread far and wide. Jesus was also a miracle worker and a healer.

God shared His love and divine power with the those He met and it left them forever changed. That's how we should be when we encounter Jesus — in His Word, in prayer, in the sacraments — forever changed.

Jesus healed the blind. **Can you put your hands over your eyes**

and then remove them to reveal your sight?

Jesus made the paralyzed walk. **Can you lie down and then stand up and jump, excited to be able to move your legs again?**

Jesus cured those with deadly diseases, and even brought the dead back to life!

Let's experience one story of Jesus' healing ministry ... there might be some words from this story you recognize from Mass!

While Jesus was in Capernaum, a town He spent time preaching in, a Roman soldier — a centurion in charge of many other soldiers — came to see Jesus. A servant whom the centurion loved was very sick, and the centurion had heard about Jesus and His miracles. He wanted to put his need before Jesus and believed that Jesus could help him and his servant, too.

When the centurion asked Jesus to heal his servant, Jesus said He would come. But the centurion then replied, "Lord, I am not worthy to have you come under my roof; but only say the word, and my servant will be healed" (Mt 8:8).

Wow! What great faith the centurion had! He knew Jesus' word was powerful enough to heal in an instant, from anywhere. Even Jesus was amazed by the centurion's faith. In that moment, the servant was healed.

Did you recognize the centurion's words? We say them every time we go to Mass, before receiving Jesus in the Eucharist! Next time we go to Mass, listen for those words and pray that you can also have a strong faith like the centurion — a faith that amazes Jesus!

Thank you, God, for the gift of Your Holy Word today.

Deep Dive: the Passion narrative in one of the Gospels, for example, Matthew 26:17–28:20

Adults: If you have wooden dolls or can print or make some characters from the Passion story, children love acting out the story as it's read!

15

Jesus, the Savior

Let's journey back to the time of Jesus' death and resurrection. All of salvation history has been building toward this moment. As the Bible tells us, "For God so loved the world that he gave his only-begotten Son, that whoever believes in him should not perish but have eternal life" (John 3:16).

What good news! God loved us so much that Jesus gave His very life for us. He paid the price for our sins so we could spend forever with Him in heaven.

On the night before He died, Jesus celebrated the Passover meal with His apostles. He took bread, blessed it and broke it, and gave it to His disciples, saying, "This is my body which is given for you. Do this in remembrance of me" (Lk 22:19).

What sacrament was Jesus establishing here? That's right, the Eucharist! We are able to eat and drink Christ's Body and Blood! He gave us this gift of His very self, a sacrament instituted for the good of His Church at the Last Supper. That night, Jesus also washed the disciples' feet **(can you pretend to wash another's feet?)** and told Peter that, sadly, before the cock crowed twice, Peter would have denied Jesus three times. **Can you crow like a rooster twice?**

Jesus prayed in the Garden of Gethsemane, uniting His will to His Heavenly Father's, and then Judas, one of His apostles, betrayed Him with a kiss. **Do you want to kiss me on the cheek like Judas kissed Jesus to identify Him to the chief priests and temple guards who arrested Him?** What a sad gesture of betrayal, one that should be a gesture of love.

From there Jesus was questioned, teased, ridiculed, scourged, and condemned to be crucified. He carried a painfully heavy wooden cross to a hill, where He died between two criminals. The earth shook **(can you stomp your feet on the ground to make**

the sound of earth rumbling?) and the veil in the Temple, hiding the holiest room, was torn from top to bottom.

Thankfully, this was not the end of the story.

On Sunday, several women went to the tomb where Jesus was buried, but to their surprise, the large stone blocking the entrance had been rolled away! An angel told them that Jesus had risen!

When Jesus saw His apostles, He told them, "Do not be afraid ... I am with you always" (Mt 28:10, 20). These are great words to end with. May we never be afraid, because Jesus, our Savior, has conquered death and is always with us! **Shout with me, "Thank you, Jesus!"**

Thank you, God, for the gift of Your Holy Word today.

Deep Dive: Acts 2

Adults: Have candles for today's story time, sitting unlit in front of each child. If you have safety concerns, electronic or paper candles will work!

16

The Age of the Church

Let's explore the age of the Church, the time period in salvation history that we are living in today! The age of the Church had an exciting beginning.

Before Jesus ascended into heaven, He promised His disciples that He would send the Holy Spirit to them.

The apostles waited together in Jerusalem on the day of Pentecost. Suddenly, "a sound came from heaven like the rush of a mighty wind" (Acts 2:2). **Can you make the sound of a big, rushing wind?** Then tongues of fire came to rest on each one of them.

Adults, light the candles now.

And Jesus' apostles were filled with the Holy Spirit. Can you imagine what that must have been like, to be in the room with the apostles, receiving the Holy Spirit on that day of Pentecost?

Immediately, the apostles could speak in different

languages, and they rushed to the streets, where they were able to share the gospel with people of all different lands and tongues. **Can you pretend to talk in a different language, one you don't even know?** I may not be able to understand you, but everyone could understand the apostles that day!

Thousands of people came to believe in Jesus and were baptized. Jesus' disciples had courage to share their faith, and we can ask the Holy Spirit for courage **(show me your muscles!)** to always live and share our Catholic faith, too.

Let's finish our story time by singing *Come, Holy Ghost* to remember this exciting time in salvation history, and then blow out the candles after we sing!

Come Holy Ghost, Creator blest
And in our hearts take up thy rest.
Come with thy grace and heav'nly aid
To fill the hearts which thou hast made,
To fill the hearts which thou hast made.

Thank you, God, for the gift of Your Holy Word today.

Helping families love and live the Catholic Faith

OSV Kids is on a mission to help children learn about, live, and love the Catholic Faith. Every OSV Kids product is prayerfully developed to introduce children of all ages to Jesus and his Church. Using beautiful artwork, engaging storytelling, and fun activities, OSV Kids products help families form and develop their Catholic identity and learn to live the faith with great joy.

MONTHLY ACTIVITY BOOK

Learn more at OSVKids.com

BOARD BOOKS

PICTURE BOOKS

MIDDLE GRADE

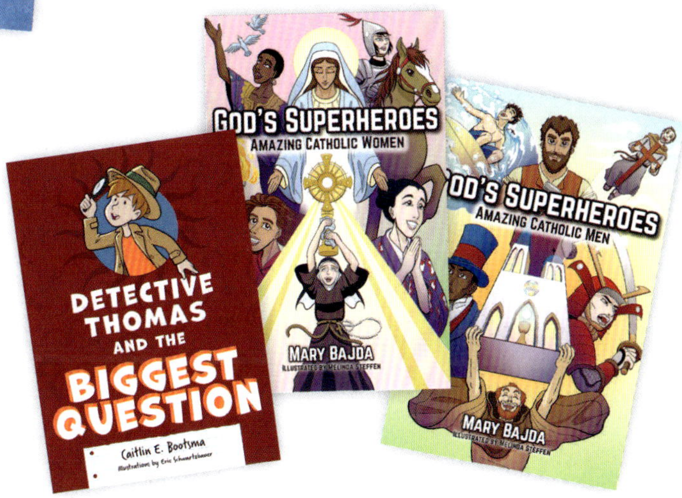

About the Author

Katie Warner is a Catholic homeschooling mom and a bestselling children's book author. Her popular titles include *Father Ben Gets Ready for Mass*, *Listening for God: Silence Practice for Little Ones*, and *Jack Giorgio: Future Priest*. She has a graduate degree in Catholic Theology and lives in Georgia with her husband and fellow book-loving children. Check out her entire children's book collection and free, fun activities for little ones at FirstFaithTreasury.com, and connect with Katie online (she loves to hear from readers!) at KatieWarner.com or @katiewarnercatholic.

About the Illustrator

Amy Rodriguez is an illustrator and digital artist based in Los Angeles, California. She creates colorful illustrations that share the joy and beauty of the Catholic faith. Amy has illustrated seven picture books, one of which received an Excellence in Publishing award from the Association of Catholic Publishers. She has worked with publishers and media groups such as TAN Books, Augustine Studios, Our Sunday Visitor, and Pauline Books and Media. Visit Amy on Instagram for her latest work: @amyrodriguez.art.